In the Animal World

Emma Serl

In the Animal World

Emma Serl

HILLSIDE EDUCATION

Cover and interior book design by Mary Jo Loboda

ISBN: 978-0-9969986-5-9

Hillside Education
475 Bidwell Hill Road
Lake Ariel, PA 18436
www.hillsideeducation.com

SERL SERIES
SUPPLEMENTARY READERS

IN THE ANIMAL WORLD

BY

EMMA SERL

AUTHOR OF

"IN FABLELAND"

ILLUSTRATED BY

HARRY E. WOOD

Acknowledgements

Acknowledgment is made to *the following p*ublishers and authors for the use of copyright material, some of which *has been adapted: The* Sunday School Times; Primary *Education, published by* the *Educational Publishing* Company; Edward Arnold, for The *Story of a Donkey;* Henry Altemus Company, for The Mother Seal's Story and Father Wolf and the Pack; Hougton Mifflin Company, *for A Night w*ith a Wolf, by Bayard Taylor; and Ella Wheeler Wilcox and her publisher, W.B. Conkey, for use of a part of the poem, Two Pussy Cats.

Contents

Flesh-Eating Animals

Plant-Eating Animals

I.
THE CAT FAMILY

THE KITTEN

See the kitten on the wall,
Sporting with the leaves that fall,
Withered leaves — one — two — and three —
From the lofty elder-tree!
Through the calm and frosty air
Of this morning bright and fair,
Eddying round and round they sink.

But the kitten, how she starts,
Crouches, stretches, paws, and darts;
First at one, and then its fellow
Just as light and just as yellow;
There are many now—now one —
Now they stop, and there are none.

—WILLIAM WORDSWORTH

7

MALTA'S BABIES

Malta had lost all her kittens, and she was very lonesome. She had hunted for them and called them, but nowhere could they be found.

She disappeared for a few days, and when she returned she carried something very carefully in her mouth. She took it to the box in the barn where her little ones had been and put it gently down. She went away again and soon returned with another little one like the first.

Now there were two babies in the box, and Malta seemed contented.

To be sure, they were not like her own little ones; these had bushy tails and bright eyes. They did not like to be washed as kittens ought, but Malta held them with her paws and scrubbed them as she thought best. Soon they were large enough to leave the box and frisk about on the floor.

One day Malta brought them a live mouse, but they did not seem to care for it. "Mew, mew," she said, "come and play with this nice mouse." But the little ones only looked at it and got out of its way when it came too

close. Malta decided that they must be very stupid kittens.

The next week she took them into the garden; she thought she would teach them how to climb a tree, but they needed no showing; up the trunk they ran in a way Malta had never seen kittens go. They frisked and frolicked among the branches until poor Malta grew frightened.

A few weeks later the squirrels left good Mother Malta and went to live in the old maple tree.

Malta watches them sometimes when she lies on the porch in the sunshine.

Such queer children she never saw. There are some things she cannot understand; it is of no use to try, so she curls herself up and takes another nap.

TWO PUSSY CATS

I

THE PET CAT

Dainty little ball of fur, sleek and round and fat,
Yawning through the lazy hours, some one's
      household cat.
Lying on a bed of down, decked in ribbons gay,
What a pleasant life you lead, whether night or day.

Romping through the house at will, racing down the
      hall,
      Full of pretty playful pranks, loved
        and praised by all.
      Wandering from room to room to find
        the choicest spot,
        Favored little house-
        hold puss, happy is
        your lot.

II

THE TRAMP CAT

Poor little beggar cat, hollow-eyed and gaunt,
Creeping down the alleyways like a ghost of want,
Kicked and beat by thoughtless boys, bent on cruel play,
What a sorry life you lead, whether night or day.

Hunting after crusts or crumbs, gnawing meatless
    bones,
Trembling at a human step, fearing bricks and stones,
Shrinking at an outstretched hand, knowing only blows,
Wretched little beggar cat, born to suffer
    woes.

— ELLA WHEELER WILCOX

ANDROCLUS AND THE LION

Long ago in the great city of Rome there lived a slave named Androclus. His master was a cruel man, and the poor slave received blows and harsh words from morning until night.

At last Androclus felt that he could stand this treatment no longer; so he ran away and hid in the forest. There he ate berries and ripe fruit, and at night he slept in a cave among the rocks.

One morning very early, he was awakened by the loud roars of a lion.

Androclus sprang up in great fright and saw the huge beast standing at the door of the cave. Again the lion roared, and the poor slave felt sure that he should be killed.

The animal came farther into the cave, and Androclus noticed that something seemed to be the matter with one of his paws. He held the foot up and whined as if in great pain.

At last Androclus took hold of the paw to look at it.

19

There in the soft part of the foot was a great thorn.

The lion seemed to know that the man in the cave could help him and held quite still for his foot to be examined. Androclus took hold of the thorn with his fingers, then gave a quick pull, and it was out. The great beast leaped about like a dog and licked the hands and face of Androclus.

The slave and the lion now lived together in the cave. They slept side by side, and often they hunted together in the wood.

But one day some soldiers found Androclus and took

him back to Rome. There he was put into prison and tried for running away from his master. He was condemned and sentenced to fight a wild animal in the arena.

The day for the fight came, and great crowds of people went to see the dreadful sight. The emperor sat on a high throne, and the seats round about were filled with thousands of eager people.

For days a great lion had been kept in a cage without food. The poor slave was brought into the arena, the doors of the cage were opened, and the hungry lion rushed forth with a roar.

Seeing the trembling man, he dashed toward him.

Then a strange thing happened. Instead of tearing the slave to pieces as the people expected, the lion paused licked the hands of Androclus, and then lay down by his side. Androclus gave a cry of gladness and threw his arms around the neck of the great beast, for it was the lion with whom he had lived in the wood!

The emperor and the people were amazed. Never before had such a sight been seen in the arena.

Then, standing before the

throne, Androclus told of his cruel master, of his flight to the wood, of the lion's hurt paw, and of the friendship between them.

When he had finished, the people cried: "Let them both go free! Let them both go free ! "

So the gates were opened, and Androclus and the lion went back to the cave on the side of the mountain.

— Aesop's Fables

THE TIGER KITTEN

Up the steep side of a mountain, within a large cave, the mother tiger had made her home. Here among the rocks, three little tiger kittens played while they waited for their mother's return.

Soon the smallest one lifted his head and listened; far away he had heard a faint call. The others stopped their play, and all three stood still. Again the cry came, and this time there was no mistaking it — the mother tiger was coming home to her little ones.

All night she had been out hunting, and now it was past time for breakfast. The kittens were hungry. They were too old for milk, and the careful mother daily brought them choice bits of food, — sometimes a young bird or perhaps a piece of a sheep that she had killed in the valley.

Nearer the cry came, and in a moment, the beautiful striped mother leaped grace-fully over the rocks and into the cave door. The little ones crowded around her, eager for the food she was bringing. This morning it was a

young rabbit, which the mother had found at the door of its burrow. How the tiger kittens fought over it! They growled and pulled, each one trying to get the largest piece. At last the meal was finished, and they lay down to rest and sleep.

Other days passed in the same way, and then the mother tiger decided to take the kittens out hunting with her. One morning she jumped from the cave to the rock below. There she stopped and called. Three little kittens looked over the edge at her and mewed, but all were afraid to jump.

Again she called, but not a kitten came. After waiting a moment the mother leaped back to the cave, and picking up one in her mouth, again jumped down. Leaving him in the grass below, she went back for a second one and placed him by his brother. She was about to go back for the third time, when the smallest kitten, who had been left in the cave, gave a little mew, then made a brave jump, and landed in the soft grass near the others.

The little family now moved quietly through the bushes, the mother tiger showing them how to creep so as not to be seen or heard.

Soon they came to the river, and there the mother made them lie still under some low trees. For a long time they watched the strange things about them. Birds were flying high in the sky, others were singing in the tree tops, and queer little animals were playing in the sunshine.

At noon some cattle came down to the river to drink. When they were quite near, the mother slipped quietly toward a young calf, made a great leap, and fastened her teeth and claws into its back. The other animals fled in fright while the tiger

dragged her prey away among the bushes. Here mother and young ones had a great feast.

The next day the smallest tiger kitten caught a fat young duck that had flown down to the water's edge. Not wishing share it, he carried it to up the bank where he could eat it alone. The others tried to follow him, but the calls of the mother took them back to her side, and the smallest one was left alone with the dinner he had so cleverly caught.

His rough little tongue stripped the flesh from the bones of the young duck and his sharp teeth tore it into shreds. It was a good meal, and when it was finished, he looked around and wished for more.

Far down in the bushes the mother tiger was calling, and he could hear the sharp cries of his brothers as they played together. But he was not ready to go back. It was warm and pleasant on the rocks in the sunshine. Here was a fine place for a sleepy kitten to take a nap. He was just about to curl himself up among some leaves and grasses when there was a sudden rush of wings above him. Sharp talons were fastened into his back, and he was borne swiftly upward through the air.

The little one gave a
startled cry of fright, but
the eagle only held him the
tighter. Higher and higher
they went over the trees
toward the eagle's nest on the
cliff above.

But in a minute the little tiger
had pulled himself partly free.
His sharp claws tore the side
of the big bird while his teeth stripped
feathers and flesh from her neck. The
eagle's hooked bill caught him by the
back of his head, but still the little fellow
fought.

Deeper and deeper went the teeth and
claws of the tiger kitten. The eagle began

to fly slower. She even tried to drop the prey she had so unwisely caught, but she could not get rid of him. More feathers fell to the ground and more flesh was torn from her body.

The great bird was growing weak and was flying downward. The tiger kitten had fastened itself upon her side below one of the big wings. With all his strength he still pulled and tore until the eagle could endure it no longer. She made one more attempt to fly and then fell in a heap to the ground.

The mother tiger had heard the cry of her little one, and from the high bank she had watched the strange fight. Quickly she came leaping through the bushes to the place where the eagle and the tiger kitten had fallen.

That night the little tiger feasted upon the flesh of the eagle. But for many days his back showed the marks made by the talons of the greatest bird of the air.

THE PANTHER
AND THE GRIZZLY

The panther stood on the ledge in front of her den and watched the sun as it rose over the tree tops.

For years the great panther had made her home in the cave, and for years she had been mistress of the mountain. The other animals, knowing of her power and cunning, rarely came near, and so, alone on the steep slope, she cared for her two little ones.

From her high rock she could see far down the valley, and her keen eyes watched for a deer or elk that might wander down to the river in search of food.

For days the snow had fallen, and the mountain and valley were covered with its soft whiteness.

Suddenly the mother panther raised her head and listened. Far down the mountain side she heard a faint sound. Quietly she moved to the edge of the rock, and her great body drew itself together for a spring. From here she

could see down the slope, but there was nothing in sight but the snow-covered rocks and bushes.

Anxiously she listened as the sounds grew louder. The steps were not those of a deer, of that she felt sure; nor could they be those of the small wood folk. But surely some one was coming. The panther was growing angry. Her tail jerked and she crouched close to the narrow ledge.

Nearer came the sounds. Now she could hear the snapping and cracking of bushes as a big body forced its way through. An enemy had dared to come to her mountain, and that enemy must be a bear!

The great panther hated bears. Many times she bad fought with them in the valley, but never before had one dared to come to her den. Her body remained rigid, but her tail lashed the ground in front of the cave. Faint cries came from the little ones inside, and she moved closer to the door of the den.

Nearer and nearer came the sounds. A moment more and a big animal lifted itself to the ledge. The mother panther gave a startled look at the great shape, — it was not one

of the black bears of the valley, but the fierce grizzly from across the river!

She crouched closer to the cave, for she well knew that she had no chance in a fight with this ferocious beast. She could easily save herself. One leap would carry her to safety, but how could she save her babies? For them she must fight even this strong, fierce foe.

The waiting panther did not stir until the grizzly was quite close. Then with a quick spring she began the fight. Her slender body leaped to and fro, but the heavy paws of the great bear shot forth with wonderful quickness. Inch by inch the grizzly forced his way to

the mouth of the den, while the mother panther fought furiously with teeth and claws.

Then suddenly both animals stopped! From above them on the side of the mountain came a sound of snapping twigs and crashing trees. The panther glared at her foe, while the bear, startled by the strange noise, sat back on his haunches and listened.

From the top of the cliff a few stones fell, more stones and snow followed, and then a great mass of snow and ice slid down, sweeping everything before it. It fell to the ledge, and carrying with it panther and grizzly, dropped to the foot of the precipice.

A moment later the panther shook the snow from her tawny sides and leaped back up the slope to her little ones. After a while the pile of snow at the foot of the cliff began to move, and soon an enormous grizzly pushed his way out of the drift, walked slowly down the valley, and crossed to the mountain on the other side.

THE CAT FAMILY

lion   leopard wild cat

tiger   puma   lynx

panther jaguar   domestic cat

The members of the cat family are graceful animals with long bodies, round heads, keen eyes, pointed ears, sharp teeth, long whiskers, and soft paws. In their paws are sharp, curved claws that can be thrust out and drawn in. Their bodies are covered with thick, soft fur. The tongues of all the animals of this group are rough; this roughness aids

them in pulling the meat from the bones of the animals they catch; it is also of use in cleaning their beautiful fur. Their food consists of smaller animals and birds. Most of these animals hunt at night, for in the dark their eyes become larger so as to take in every ray of light.

The lion is called the King of Beasts because of its great strength and also because it is not afraid to attack any other animal. Its color is a tawny yellow, lighter on the under parts of the body and darker above. The lion when full grown has a thick, shaggy mane of long hair, which grows from the neck and shoulders. The tip of the tail is decorated with a tuft of dark hair. The lioness is not so large as her mate and has no mane. Lions are found in Africa and the warm countries of Asia.

The tiger is almost as large as the lion. Its body is nearly covered with black and yellow stripes. Like the lion, it makes its home in the jungles of Asia and Africa.

The panther and leopard are not so large as the tiger. Their bodies are covered with dark spots. They are able to climb trees; there, hidden among the branches, they watch for their prey and spring upon it as it passes on the ground beneath them. The panther is to be found in parts of America. The leopard lives in Asia and Africa.

The puma is called the American lion. Its shrill scream may sometimes be heard in the mountains of the west. Like the leopard and the panther, it springs upon its prey from the branches of trees. Unlike most of the other members of this group, it is not satisfied with catching a single animal, but when meeting a herd of cattle or a flock of sheep it will kill as many as it can, sucking a little blood from each one. It has been known to kill fifty sheep in one night.

The jaguar is in many respects like the leopard. Its golden yellow coat is marked with dark spots. It is strong and fierce, and often attacks animals much larger than itself. It is found in unsettled parts of America.

The wild cat is larger than the domestic cat. It was once common in the thick woods of America, but is now to be found only in the thinly settled parts. It is ferocious and kills large numbers of small animals and birds.

The lynx is less fierce than most of the other animals of this group. It hunts hares, rabbits, and other small prey. Its fur forms a valuable article of commerce. The lynx is found in Europe and in the northern and western parts of the United States.

The domestic cat is a pet in many homes. It is clean in its habits and is less noisy than the dog. It is affectionate, and often shows surprising intelligence.

II.
THE DOG FAMILY

LASSIE, THE SHEPHERD'S DOG

Away up in the mountains there lived a father and mother and Paul, a dear little boy, not quite four years old.

The father was a shepherd, and every day with the help of his faithful dog, Lassie, he cared for a large flock of sheep that fed on the fresh grass in the valley.

Each morning when Lassie and the father started to take the sheep to their pasture, the little fellow cried to go too.

"See how he wants to go with you," said the

mother. "When he is older, he will help you care for the sheep."

"Let me take him today," said the father. "We shall not go far. If he gets tired, Lassie can carry him on her back."

So the mother packed a lunch, and the three started down the valley, driving the sheep before them.

The sun shone and the air was bright and warm.

How happy little Paul was! He laughed and talked as he held to his father's hand or sometimes rode on his shoulder. At noon they ate their lunch by the side of the river that flowed

through the valley. Then the father spread his coat upon the ground, and the little boy slept in the shade of a big tree. When he awoke, the sun was not shining, clouds had spread over the sky, and a fog was settling down in the valley.

"We must take the sheep home," said the shepherd. "There is going to be a storm." Calling Lassie, he sent her to collect the scattered flock.

"My son," the father said, "you must wait here by this big tree. When the sheep are together, I will come and carry

you home. Now be sure not to move away from this place."

"All right, Father," was the answer, and the shepherd went back to his sheep.

Soon the fog grew thicker and darker. The rain began to fall, and the lightning flashed. Some of the sheep had wandered far away, and the shepherd had trouble in finding them. At last the father returned for his little son. He easily found the big tree, but no boy was near it. "Paul, O Paul," he called, but no answer came except the crash of the thunder. Greatly frightened, the anxious father searched

first in one direction, then in another. Surely the little fellow could not have gone far. The river in the valley was rapidly rising. What if the boy had fallen in!

Up the valley he could hear the sharp barks of Lassie as she drove the sheep. Perhaps the child had followed her home. Paul and Lassie were good friends; he must have seen the dog as she passed with the sheep.

Eagerly the father ran toward his home, feeling sure that he would find the boy there. When he reached the cottage, the mother was standing at the door waiting for them, but no little Paul was by her side.

Together the frightened par-
ents went out into the storm
to search for their little son.
Back and forth, all night,
they wandered through
the valley.

"I don't see where Lassie
can be," said the father. "If
she were only here, she
might help us."

The mother told how
Lassie had brought the sheep home, and how
together they had driven them into the fold.
Then as soon as the sheep were safe inside,
Lassie had disappeared and had not been seen
since.

Next morning while the father went to ask the neighbors to help him. the tired mother returned alone to the cottage. As she sat crying in their little home, suddenly she heard the bark of Lassie. Quickly the woman ran to the door and let the dog in.

"Poor Lassie!" she cried. "How tired you look! You must be hungry too. Do you want something to eat?"

Two sharp barks were the answer, and the woman placed on the floor part of a loaf of bread. Without stopping to eat it, Lassie seized it in her mouth and ran away.

"How strange!" said the woman. "I never knew Lassie to act that way before."

Neighbors did not live near, and it was almost noon before the father returned with two men to help him. All day they searched through the valley and up the mountain side, but no trace of the lost boy did they find.

That evening Lassie again came to the house and begged for something to eat. When food was given her, she picked it up as before and dashed away with it.

"I wish we had gone with the dog," said one of the men. "Perhaps she could find the boy."

Next morning the dog came again for food, and as she left the father followed her. Lassie carried the bread in her mouth, but this time she trotted slowly ahead of her master.

Down the valley the dog went, straight to the big tree. There she turned toward the bank of the river. Climbing over the steep cliff, she jumped to a large rock below.

The shepherd followed her with difficulty, but when he reached the space below, a strange sight met his eyes. There in a cave, back of the big rock, was Lassie. Sitting on the ground near her, eating the bread she had brought, was the lost boy.

The little fellow must have wandered from the big tree, and in the dark rolled over the cliff to the rock below. The swift water of the river in front of him and the steep

cliff behind had kept him in the cave. Here Lassie had found him, and here she had cared for him.

Soon in the little cottage on the mountain side the happy mother held her son in one arm, while the other clasped the neck of Lassie, the faithful dog.

A MATTER OF TRUTHFULNESS

Early one morning, Mark Lewis was awakened by a low whining under his window.

He jumped quickly out of bed and ran to the open window. He looked out, and there by the side of the house he saw a brown and white puppy.

Mark hurried down and opened the door. The little dog came in quickly, glad to get near a warm stove once more. In a minute his cold black nose was deep in a dish of milk, and it

did not come out until the last drop was gone.

Mark and his brothers, Fred and Charlie, begged so hard to keep the dog that at last Mother said they might. The boys gave him the name of Bob and began at once to teach him some tricks.

A few days later they were playing with him in front of the house. Mark had a ball which he threw for Bob to chase. Sometimes he thought it was better fun not to throw the ball but only to make the motion. Then the children would laugh at Bob's effort to find it.

While they were playing in this way. the doctor drove along and stopped to see what they were doing. When he had watched a few minutes, he called them to his carriage and said: "Boys, I am sorry to see that you are lying to your dog. He has only a small dog's mind. He cannot think things out for himself as you can. When you make a motion as if to throw the ball, he trusts you. He thinks you mean to throw it, and when you do not throw it, you really tell him a lie. By and by, he will learn that he cannot trust you, and then he will not do what you tell him to. You ought never to lie to a dog."

This seemed funny to the boys at first, but they all liked the doctor and so they stopped fooling Bob. In time he became so well trained that he would do anything his young masters told him to do, if only he could understand what they meant.

Best of all he liked to bring things out of the water. When the boys sent him in, Bob was sure to find there something that should be brought to land.

As the months passed, Bob grew to be a big dog, the constant friend and play-fellow of the children.

One afternoon in summer they all went down to the edge of

the pond. While Mark and Charlie were playing, little Fred climbed on to a big rock that reached out into deep water. All at once there was a splash and a scream, and Fred was gone. He had slipped from the rock!

The boys ran down the bank, but Fred was nowhere to be seen. In their fear both screamed as loud as they could. A second later Bob came running through the bushes, barking as much as to say: "What is the matter? Do you want me?"

Instantly both boys had the same thought. Bob could do what they could not. Each made the motion of throwing something into the water and cried, "In, Bob, in! Go fetch it!"

With a great splash Bob leaped clear of the rock, and began to swim in a circle. He had not made even one turn when Fred's head came up near him. The dog did not have to be told what to do. He knew that he was there to get something, so he fastened his teeth in the child's coat collar, and in half a minute had pulled him into

shallow water where his brothers could drag him out.

That evening when the doctor came, he was told how Fred had been saved. He patted Bob's head tenderly, and then turning to the boys he said, "Now, do you see why it is best never to lie to a dog? "

A NIGHT WITH A WOLF

Little one, come to my knee !
    Hark how the rain is pouring
Over the roof, in the pitch-black night,
    And the wind in the woods a-roaring!

Hush, my darling, and listen,
    Then pay for the story with kisses ;
Father was lost in the pitch-black night,
    In just such a storm as this is.

High up in the lonely mountains,
    Where the wild men watched and waited,
Wolves in the forest and bears in the bush,
    And I on my path belated.

I crept along in the darkness,
     Stunned and bruised and blinded —
Crept to a fir with thick-set boughs,
     And a sheltering rock behind it.

There, from the blowing and raining,
     Crouching, I sought to hide me;
Something rustled, two green eyes shone,
     And a wolf lay down beside me.

Little one, be not frightened:
     I and the wolf together,
Side by side, through the long, long
          night,
Hid from the awful weather.

His wet fur pressed against me;
     Each of us warmed the other ;
Each of us felt in the stormy dark,
     That beast
     and man was
     brother.

And when the falling forest
　　No longer crashed in warning,
Each of us went from our hiding-place
　　Forth in the wild, wet morning.

Darling, kiss me in payment;
Hark, how the wind is roaring;
　　Father's house is a better place
When the stormy rain is pouring.

— BAYARD TAYLOR

FATHER WOLF AND THE PACK

It was very cold. The streams were covered with ice, and the whole land was white with snow.

The wolves were hungry. They had not had anything to eat for days and days.

"When shall we have some dinner, Father?" whines the little wolves.

"Please bring us something to eat; we are so hungry."

And Grayfur, the poor father wolf, didn't know what to say.

That evening as they were all lying close together, trying to keep warm, there came a long, low howl from one of the neighbor wolves. This was answered by another wolf, and then by another, and another. Even the little ones knew what it meant; it was the gathering of the pack.

Grayfur started out and went toward the forest to meet the other wolves. They seemed to come from every direction, and soon there was a large number talking and growling together. All were hungry and eager to be off on the hunt.

Presently a large wolf, the leader of the pack, stepped forward. "Brothers," he said, "are you hungry?"

What a howl there was, to be sure!

"Then follow me," was the answer.

He turned and began to trot slowly through the woods. The other wolves threw up their heads and yelped for joy as they bounded after him.

Grayfur wondered where they were going. After a time they left the woods and were out in the open fields. The old leader kept up a steady trot across the snow, and the pack followed as closely as they could.

Grayfur had never been so far away from the forest before. What could they be going to catch?

Presently the old leader stopped and sniffed at the ground, then threw up his head, howled, and started on again. Grayfur sniffed the ground too, and found a little hole in the snow, then another, and another, and then a long line of them. He knew what they were; they were the footsteps of men! It was a road, and the old leader was taking them to a village!

Grayfur understood now that they were going

to attack the village; perhaps they might find something to eat, but it was very bold. He had never done such a thing before. However, he thought to himself that there were a good many others with him; so he ran on. He was very hungry, and so were his little ones at home.

After they had gone on a little farther, the old leader stopped, and all the other wolves gathered around him. "Now," he said, "each one must find his dinner for himself. Over there in the village are sheep and goats and pigs and chickens, but remember there are

also men and dogs! Let each one go his own way and find what he can!" Then he darted off like a shot and was lost in the darkness.

Grayfur stopped a moment; then he too set off. He ran until he came close to a cottage, where he saw a light burning in a window. Quietly he crept around the house; at the back he found a pen in which were sheep crowded close together.

"Here is my dinner," said Grayfur to himself, and in less than no time he had jumped over the fence and was among the sheep.

Just then from the front of the house there came the loud barking of dogs and the shouting of men. Soon the whole village was awake and everyone was looking after his property.

But Grayfur was off by this time, running home as fast as he could go; and that evening the little wolves had a fat young lamb for dinner.

A TRAP

At the foot of a hill near the bank of the river, there lived three young foxes.

Their mother had left them and had made a home for herself far down the valley. For several months she had cared for them and brought food to them, but now she knew that they were large enough to look out for themselves.

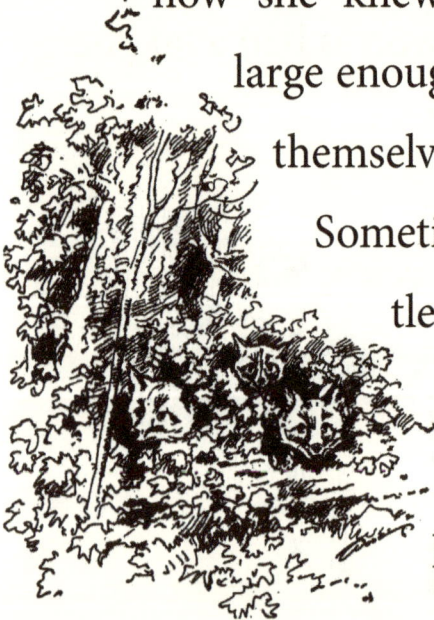

Sometimes the three little foxes slept in the hollow log near the door of their home, sometimes they played among the bushes, and every night they hunted in the woods and fields near by.

Often they were hungry, for it was not always easy to find a dinner; and then, sometimes, they had more than enough to eat.

One evening as the largest one started out, he ran straight toward the river. There the wild ducks and other water birds made their nests among the weeds and rushes. They were not hard to catch, and many a choice meal had the young fox eaten there.

But this night not a duck could he find. Once he caught the smell of some kind of bird, and followed it for a short distance only to find an empty nest. The bird had flown.

He went still farther down the bank, but no dinner was in sight. Then turning, he ran up the hill and through a field of grain on the other side. A field mouse ran across his path. He stopped and caught it; a few feet farther he caught another. They were good, but not enough for a hungry fox.

At the edge of the field he found a rabbit sitting near the door of its home. That would be a fine feast if he could get it. Slyly the fox crept through the bushes, but just as he was ready for a great spring, the rabbit leaped into its burrow. In vain the fox dug in the ground with his strong claws; no rabbit did he get.

Still hungry, he turned again toward the river. Suddenly he stopped. Surely he caught the scent of fresh meat! He ran rapidly in the direction of the good smell. Soon he was close to the river, and with every step the scent grew stronger and better.

A few more jumps and the hungry fox saw a fine

piece of juicy meat fastened to the twig of a tree.

Here was a splendid meal, but the fox stopped. Something did not seem just right. Slowly he walked in a circle around the tempting morsel. He wanted it more and more and yet he was afraid.

Round and round he went in the bushes, his nose close to the ground. There was no trace of anything wrong there, no smell of anything but the good fresh meat.

He jumped to the bank below and carefully examined the stones. Near one of them he stopped. Here was a different scent. Again and again the fox sniffed the ground. Then he turned from the tempting smell and walked slowly away—for near the stone was the trace of a man's foot! Though the fox was young, he well knew the meaning of that smell. That fine fresh meat was only the bait of a trap which the man had carefully placed in the bushes.

The fox leaped over the stones, and, as he ran up the hill in the moonlight, he seemed to laugh at the man.

THE DOG FAMILY

wolf   jackal   coyote

fox   dog

The animals of the dog family have thick coats of hair, strong jaws, and long, sharp teeth. Their sense of smell is keen, and they are able to follow the scent of an animal for a long distance. The animals of the cat family use both teeth and claws in catching their prey, but these animals can bite so much harder that they do not need the help of sharp claws.

The wolf looks much like a large, shaggy dog. Wolves sometimes hunt in

packs; they are then fearless and danger-
ous. They are found in all the northern
countries of the world.

The fox is not so large
or strong as the wolf. It is
an enemy of the farmer
because of the many chickens
it kills. The fur of some kinds of foxes is
very valuable.

The coyote, or prairie wolf, is about
one third smaller than the gray wolf, but
in form and color they are much alike.
The food of the coyote consists of rabbits, prairie dogs, hares, and other small
animals.

The jackal is a little larger than the
fox. It is found in some parts of Asia and

Africa. It often follows larger animals and eats the parts of their prey which they may leave.

The dog is the friend, companion, and helper of man. Dogs have been taught to search for persons lost in the snow, they aid their masters in hunting, they have many times saved people from drowning, and are of great help to shepherds in caring for sheep. In cold countries, dogs are used to draw sledges and are able to travel long distances over the ice and snow.

III.
SEALS AND SEA LIONS

THE MOTHER SEAL'S STORY

Far away up in the north, midst the ice and snow, there lived a family of seals —a father seal, a mother seal, and a little baby seal.

The baby seal swam about in the water and had all sorts of games with the other little seals who lived close by. Sometimes he climbed up on to the rocks, and then as he lay by his mother's side, she told him stories of what happened to her when she was a little seal. The story he

liked best of all was what he called the "Man Story."

He used to say to his mother, "Tell me the Man Story again, Mother."

And his mother would say, "Why, I've told you that so many times, dear; wouldn't you like a new story?"

But the little seal would answer, "No, I want the Man Story, Mother. I like that best."

Then the mother seal would begin, "Long, long ago, when I was a little baby seal—"

"As little as I, Mother?" the little seal would ask.

"Yes, smaller than you are now, my dear," the mother would reply. "I used to live here with my father and mother, and one day as we were swimming about in the sea, we saw a great big thing like a rock, with wings, come sailing along on the top of the water. I learned afterwards that it was called a ship. It came nearer and nearer; then it stopped, and a little thing called a boat was let down into the water. It came swimming along toward us, and we heard the most beautiful

music coming from it. Now, you know we all like music very much; so we swam nearer to the boat to listen. When we got quite close, we saw that there were some funny-looking creatures sitting in it."

"Oh, those were men, weren't they, Mother?" the little seal would say.

"Yes, dear," the mother seal would answer. "They seemed to be quite  friendly, and they made the sweet music for us. But that night we noticed that some of our friends were missing, and we did not know what had become of them. A few days later my mother did not come home. She had been out to listen to the music. We waited and waited, but she did not come back. The next day I heard that she would never come home any more. She had been taken away by those men; it was they who had caught all our friends. Some of them had been killed—it seemed that the men wanted their skins to make extra skins for themselves—and others had been taken alive and shut up in the ship. They had captured my mother— I am glad to say she wasn't killed—and put her on the ship with a large number of seals and sea

lions. They were all carried away to the far, far south."

"And what did the men do with them there, Mother?" the little seal would ask, though he knew the answer quite well.

"They took them away to a far country," replied the mother seal, "and put them in a sort of cage. I believe they were well treated. They were given water to swim in and fish to eat, and they were taught all sorts of tricks, but they were not free and happy as they once were."

"Is that all the Man Story, Mother?" the little seal would say.

"Yes, dear," the mother always answered. "The men haven't come again, and if they did, we should know better now, and shouldn't go near them to be caught."

"No," the little seal would say, "I shall never be caught by men."

SEALS AND SEA LIONS

seal   walrus   sea lion

These animals are formed like fish, and their limbs and feet resemble fins. Their bodies are covered with two layers of soft fur, which protect them from the icy water in which they spend much of their time. In the water they swim and dive with great swiftness, but on land they move slowly and awkwardly. The seal is found on the coast of Iceland and in other cold countries. Its head looks like that of a

big dog. Its food consists of fish, which it catches while swimming in the water. The seal is hunted for its fine fur. Its flesh is used for food, and the fat furnishes oil for the lamps of the Eskimos.

The walrus is much like the seal in shape, but it has two long tusks that grow from its upper jaw and extend downward. From these tusks some of the finest ivory is obtained. Its prey consists of small seals, fish, shrimps, and other animal life found in the sea.

The sea lion has upon its neck and shoulders a heavy mass of stiff curly hair which, because it resembles the mane of a lion, has given the creature its name.

Like the walrus, it feeds upon small seals and fish.

IV.
BEARS

BABY BLACK BEAR

For many weeks the little black bear lived in the cave, lying close to the side of his big mother. Outside, the ground was covered with snow and ice. The wind blew and the air was stinging cold. But inside the cave, cuddled in his mother's warm fur, the baby knew little of the winter weather.

Once in a while the mother awoke and licked the little one with her warm, soft tongue, as he lay by her side or tumbled around in the dry leaves. Then they both slept again, waiting for the warm days of spring.

At last one morning, the mother bear stirred uneasily. Light was coming through the doorway, which had been closed all winter by a huge snowdrift.

The big black bear was hungry. Slowly she rose and looked out on the world she had left last fall. She turned to the baby. He was still asleep in his bed of leaves and grass. So she slipped quietly from the den and climbed up the mountain, looking for breakfast. Among the bushes she caught a young rabbit; it was not a large meal for a hungry bear, but she returned to the den, and

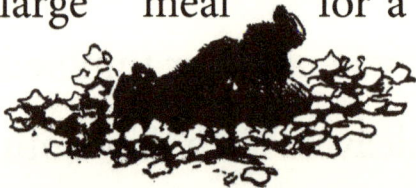

with the little one at her side, again went to sleep.

Every few days Mother Bear went out for food, while the baby remained at home.

At last the snow was gone, the hills were covered with green grass, and many ani-mals were enjoying the warm sunshine. Then Mother Bear thought that it was time to take her cub out for a walk.

The little one followed her timidly as she coaxed him from the cave. How strange and bright everything seemed! He stayed close to his mother's heels for a few steps, then went back to the cave, sat down by the door, and whined.

Mother Bear made queer grunting sounds which meant: "Don't be afraid, Baby Bear. Nothing shall hurt you while Mother is here." Baby Bear took a few steps, then a few more, and he was again by his mother's side. Slowly they made their way down the mountain, for the little one often sat down to rest.

Mother Bear now began to teach him some of the ways of the world. In the sweet tufts of grass were little snails, which she showed him how to find. With her big paws she raised up stones and turned over logs, under which the little cub found delicious ants and bugs.

It was a happy day, and at night Mother Bear lay down by an old log, while a tired baby bear cuddled up beside her and slept.

Then followed many happy days. After a while the straw-berries were ripe. Then snails and ants were forgotten, and the little one climbed the hills with his mother hunting for the sweet red fruit. After the strawber-ries were gone, they found huckleberries and sometimes a few blackberries. The woodland seemed to be filled with good things for hungry bears.

One day Mother Bear stopped by the side of a big tree and gave a few queer grunts which meant: "Come quick! Here is something to eat better than anything you have ever tasted." The little fellow came at once, tumbling down and rolling part way in his haste to answer that call. At the foot of the hill was Mother Bear, standing with her paw in a hole in the side of the tree. Baby Bear tried to put his paw in too, but just then a queer insect lighted on his nose and stung him. How it hurt! He put his two little

paws over his face
and howled and
howled.

"Never mind," grunted
Mother Bear. "Here! Eat this."
And she let him lick off the
paw that she had drawn out of
the tree.

Baby Bear stopped crying and licked
the sweet stuff until it was all gone; then
he smacked his lips and whined for more.

Mother Bear taught him to put his little paw inside the tree and pull out the
honey for himself. To be sure the bees
stung him, but that did not matter so long
as he could reach their sweet treasure.

After that, Mother Bear showed him how to find other bee trees and how to gnaw away the wood if he could not at once reach the comb.

One day, Baby Bear smelled a strange smell. Mother Bear was eating berries, so he thought he would hunt by himself. Up the mountain he went, his head close to the ground, following the scent that was different from anything his baby nose had ever smelled before. Once he lost the trail, but after wandering around he found it again, and now he was coming nearer and nearer to something he knew must be good to eat. A climb up a steep bank, and there at the top was a stick with a piece of fat bacon on the end of it. It was almost too high for Baby Bear to reach, but he sniffed at it, and was just about to give a little jump for it when Mother Bear suddenly came through the bushes. She was up the bank in a moment, and her big paw struck Baby on the side of the head with such force that he tumbled and rolled away from the good-smelling meat. Again and again she cuffed him until he whined and bowled with pain. Then in bear language she told him that

the scent he liked so well came from the bait of a trap. "You must never, never, never touch anything like that," she said.

In autumn the frost came and nuts covered the ground. Both bears ate until they could eat no more, and their bodies were covered with thick layers of fat. The days began to grow shorter, the wind blew the leaves from the trees, and the birds flew away to the warm southland.

Then Mother Bear gave her little one to understand that he must take care of himself.

One day in the thick woods he found a hollow tree close by the side of a big rock. He crawled into it and found that it was just large enough to hold his black, furry body.

Soon the snow fell and the cold days came, but safe and warm in his snug little home, Baby Bear slept all winter.

BEARS

polar bear   black bear   grizzly bear

Bears have heavy bodies covered with long, coarse hair; they have short legs, and broad, flat feet with blunt claws. They eat not only flesh but vegetable food as well. They are found in almost all countries and are fitted by nature to inhabit the hottest as well as the coldest parts of the world.

The polar bear or white bear lives in the cold north countries. Its body is covered with heavy white fur. Because of this white coat it can easily hide among the snowdrifts and ice. It has great power in swimming and diving and often pursues and kills its prey under water. Its food consists of fish and seals, and it sometimes catches even the walrus.

The black bear is found in the Rocky Mountains. It usually sleeps during the cold months of winter in a cave or hollow tree. It eats berries, roots, insects, fish, eggs, birds, and small animals.

The grizzly bear is large and powerful, and is one of the most ferocious animals of North America. Because of its great strength it is able to carry off an animal as large as a deer.

V.
GNAWERS

THE BEAVERS

The beavers were moving. For many years they had lived on the banks of a stream where they had built a fine dam, but this summer there had been no rain and the bed of the brook had become dry. Little by little the pool of water back of the dam had dried up until there was no place for the beavers to swim and play.

"We must move," said the oldest father beaver. "We must find some place where we can have water."

That night the big beavers and the little beavers started down the dry bed of the stream. Very slowly they went, for beavers swim much more easily than they walk.

After what seemed a long journey to the young ones, they reached the river into which their own little stream had emptied. They swam for about two miles, and then the big father beaver stopped. He had chosen the place for their new home.

Tired from their long trip, they rested all the next day, but when night came they were ready for work. Part of them swam a short distance up stream to a place where many young trees grew near the bank.

They climbed over the stones and began cutting down the trees by gnawing them with their sharp teeth. Soon one tree fell into the water. Quickly the branches and leaves were taken off, and it began to float down the river where the others were waiting. There the young ones stripped off the bark to save it for winter food. The older beavers pulled the log to its place where the dam was to be built and piled stones and mud upon it. Other sticks and

logs came floating down, and these also were put into place.

Thus they toiled for many nights until the work was finished, and the big father beaver said it was the best dam he had ever seen.

Back of it was a fine pool, and here the houses of sticks and mud were built. Each little house had two rooms: a bedroom upstairs and a store-room below, with the doorway under water.

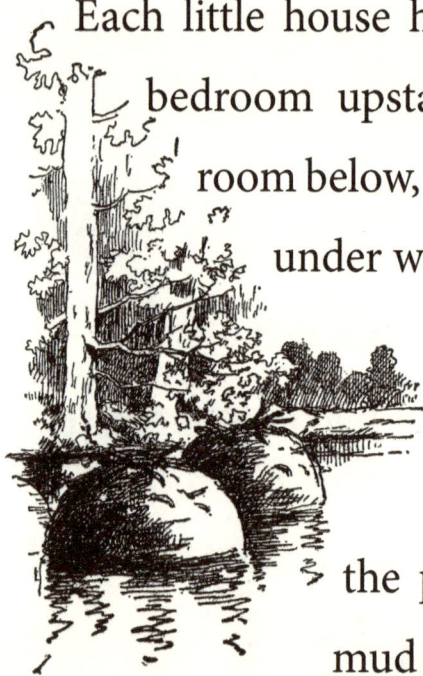

Winter came, and ice covered the surface of the pool. It froze the mud walls and closed the cracks of the beaver's homes. Inside the little rooms, snugly wrapped in their warm coats of fur, the beavers spent the long months until spring called them.

RED SQUIRREL

Red Squirrel and his mate lived in the hollow elm tree near the orchard. During the fall they had searched for acorns, other nuts, and seeds and had carried them into their snug little home, but the snow had come early and had stopped their work long before they had gathered enough. Woods and fields were covered with a soft white blanket, hiding the food which they wished to store away for the long winter time.

The days grew colder, and the squirrels slept in their hollow tree. Once in a while they woke up and ate from their scanty store; then, lying close together to keep warm, they slept again.

A month passed, and nothing remained of the seeds and nuts but a few dry shells. Red Squirrel ventured out to look about, but he found only snow and ice and bare trees. He ran up the branches of the elm and jumped over into the big oak. There a few half-frozen birds were chirping; they too had been looking for food, but all the seed plants were buried beneath the

heavy white covering. A rabbit leaped from its burrow and looked for some tender twigs or roots, but finding nothing he returned to his home under the hazel bushes.

Red Squirrel scampered up the branches of the oak, hoping that a few acorns might have been left on some of the twigs. But the strong wind had shaken them all out of their tiny cups, and still hungry, he went back to his hole in the elm.

Days passed, and the squirrels were nearly starved. Red Squirrel sometimes ran up and down the tree, but his mate lay in the nest too weak to move.

The sun shone and tried to melt the thick blanket, but the cold wind brought more gray clouds across the sky and they sent more snow to the frozen ground.

One day, as Red Squirrel was running among the branches, he noticed something strange near the orchard gate. A boy and a girl were coming toward the big elm. The boy had a basket with something in it, and the girl carried a broom.

Greatly frightened, Red Squirrel hurried into his hole, where he hid among the sticks and dry leaves. Soon strange noises could be heard outside

the tree. He listened and at last, growing bolder, he climbed up and peeped
out. What he saw made his eyes sparkle
while his tail jerked and twitched with
excitement.

Down at the foot of the tree the boy
had swept away the snow, and on the
bare ground the girl was scatter-
ing corn and wheat, bread
crumbs and cake, and yes
—Red Squirrel was sure of
it—there were a few nuts.
He was so surprised that he
forgot to be afraid, and in
his eagerness he ran part
way down the trunk.

But other little people of the woods were watching too. Bright eyes looked from the tree tops and peeped from homes in the ground and in hollow trees. When the table was set and everything was ready, the children stepped back by the fence to see what would happen.

Red Squirrel slipped down the tree a little nearer, then he ran around the trunk and peeped at the good nuts. Soon a sparrow braver than the others went down to the table and began pecking at the cake. A hungry blue jay flew down, and grabbing a kernel of corn went back to the tree top. A timid gray rabbit hopped over to a piece of bread and eagerly began to eat.

Red Squirrel on the other side of the tree trunk watched the children, but as they did not move, he went nearer and nearer to the good things. Then, making a quick jump, he picked up one of the nuts in his mouth and in a moment was back up the tree and into the hole to his hungry mate. Leaving the precious food by her side, he ran back again to the feast.

The other little animals and birds had become less afraid, and in a short time the table was entirely cleared, but not before Red Squirrel had carried several nuts and some grains of corn to his nest.

Day after day the children came, bringing good things for their hungry guests. The little people of the wood soon became so tame that it was hardly possible to brush away the snow, so eager were they for their dinner. Every day Red Squirrel watched from his hole until the gate was opened. Then closely followed by his little mate, he scampered down the tree, ran about the table, and sometimes even climbed into the basket to help himself.

So passed the weeks until the sun and the

warm south wind drove the snow away. Then the children closed their boarding house, but often during the spring and summer they came to see their little friends of the woodland.

DICK AND THE WHEEL

I do not know which Frank thought the more of, his bicycle or Dick.

The bicycle he had bought with his own money, and Dick was a little gray squirrel which his uncle had given him for a birthday present.

Frank had taught Dick many tricks. He would say, "Dick, let me see you crack this nut," and Dick would sit up on his hind legs, hold the nut in his paws, and crack it with his teeth.

There was nothing Dick liked so much as to sit on Frank's shoulder when he rode his wheel. How his little bead eyes would shine as he lay on his master's shoulder. If Frank rode slowly, then Dick would sit upright, with his long plumy tail curled up behind him, or he would sometimes skip down to the handle bars and ride there.

One morning last summer, Frank came into the house and called: "Dick! where are you? Don't you want to take a ride?"

Dick jumped from behind the door, ran out on to the porch, and seated himself on the wheel, as much as to say, "If you please." His master laughed heartily, and off they started.

They had a fine time until they went down a long hill on the way home. Here a sharp rock threw Frank from his wheel. He was not hurt, but when he scrambled to his feet, Dick was nowhere to be found.

Up and down the street Frank went, whistling and calling, but no squirrel appeared. He looked up in the trees, down in the gutter, and over the fence in the pasture. It was the strangest thing how Dick could have disappeared so suddenly!

For nearly an hour Frank searched, but it was of no use, and so at last he rode sadly home.

A happy thought came! Perhaps he would find Dick at the house. But neither his mother nor his sister had seen anything of the squirrel.

"He must have gone back to the woods," said Frank in a husky voice. Tears came into his eyes, and he reached into his pocket for his handkerchief.

How he jumped as he touched something soft and furry, and then—Dick leaped right out of the pocket on to the table! He sat up on his hind feet and blinked his funny little eyes as much as to say: "What in the world is all this fuss about? Such a fall as that, Master Frank, was too much for me. I jumped into your pocket, and it has taken me all this time to get over that tumble."

THE LITTLE RABBIT'S ESCAPE

The little rabbit was tired of his home at the end of the burrow. All his short life had been spent with his four brothers and sisters in that little nest made of dry grass and lined with bunches of his mother's soft fur.

Mother Bunny had left all the little ones asleep that morning when she went out to look for food, but this little one had waked up before the others. He raised his head and listened to the sounds he heard outside.

He was the largest and strongest rabbit in the nest. Once he had hopped to the end of the burrow where the light was, but Mother Bunny had found him there and bad driven him back.

The sounds that came from the big world were faint and seemed far away. He felt that he must go where he could hear better, and he wanted to see the wonderful things outside. Quietly he hopped along the passageway until a great light shone in his eyes.

How warm and fine it was there in the doorway, and what queer sounds came from all around. He stood up on his hind feet,

raised his long ears, and listened.

The wind blew and the leaves made soft music, birds sang in the branches, and crickets chirped in the grass. All was new and wonderful and strange to the little rabbit. He went outside the door just a little way. There he could hear and see better. A squirrel chattered from the top of a tall tree and dropped an acorn near him. He hopped quickly back into the burrow, but after waiting a few minutes he again hopped outside, this time venturing farther.

A big toad jumped near and looked at him with his big eyes. A robin sat on a fence and chirped at him, but the little rabbit was not afraid. Everything seemed to be coaxing him away from his home. Every minute in this new world was making him braver. He found some fresh green grass and something seemed to tell him that this was good to eat. He tried it and found that he wanted more. He ate a while, then paused to listen to the strange sounds.

Suddenly he noticed a different noise, such a queer rustling sound. Something was moving very softly yet swiftly in the bushes. A great fear came to the little rabbit. Here was danger! He must get back

home at once. He gave two wild leaps and then stopped, while the very life seemed to go out of his little body. Between him and the burrow was a long, spotted creature with a narrow head and two bright, cruel eyes! As these eyes looked at him, the little rabbit sank to the ground close to the side of an overhanging rock.

Slowly the snake glided nearer, while the rabbit could do nothing but look at those strange, dreadful eyes. Closer to the rock he pressed his little body; already be could hear the hiss of the

snake as the poisonous fangs were darted toward him, and then — a shadow passed over the ground.

The snake stopped suddenly and raised his head. He knew the meaning of that swiftly moving shadow. He turned as though in search of a place to hide, but he was not quick enough. From the sky above came a flash of black wings, and into the back of the snake, sharp talons were fastened. Another moment, and the hawk had carried her prey to a nest in the tree top.

Then a trembling little rabbit hopped back into the burrow on the side of the bill, where he sank down too weak to move, and there Mother Bunny found him when she came home that night.

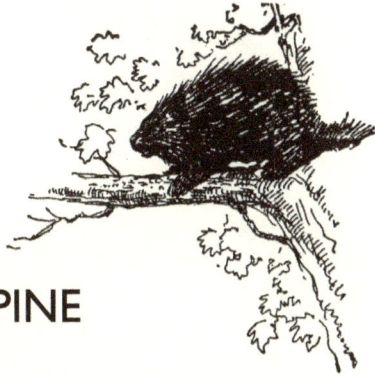

THE PORCUPINE

All day the little porcupine had
been asleep in the hollow log where he
made his home, but as soon as the sun
went down, he awoke, stretched himself,
and wished for something to eat.

He pushed his way through the narrow
opening that served as a doorway and
looked about him. It was growing dark,
just the time for him to get his supper.

Slowly and clumsily he climbed up the
hillside, the spines on his tail rattling as

he went. He found ripe straw-berries growing in the grass, while in the bushes were tender stems and twigs. What more could a young porcupine ask for a meal?

A brook that ran nearby seemed to sing, "Come and drink", but the porcupine did not notice. Little cared he for water when juicy fruit was near.

Just as he was reaching for a fine big berry, a sound of snapping twigs was heard. The porcupine stopped, raised his sharp little ears, and listened. Some animal was coming through the bushes!

He was too far away to hide in his hollow log, and his legs were too short for running. There was but one thing to do. Quickly he curled himself up in a round ball and thrust out the sharp quills that covered his body.

A moment later a large gray fox jumped through the bushes. The little porcupine lay without moving, while the fox walked slowly around him. The gray fox had seen such animals before, and he knew that it would not be wise to try to touch one. Still, the smell was good, and the fox was hungry. Carefully he gave the prickly ball a push with his foot. Then there was a howl of pain, and the fox leaped

away with some sharp spines in the soft part of his paw.

When the danger was gone, the porcupine drew the quills back into their hiding place, uncurled his soft little body, and went slowly back into the woods. There he hunted for tender roots until he again heard sounds of snapping twigs.

Again the quills came out, and a prickly ball lay on the ground, as a big black bear and her cub came down the hillside. The baby bear followed the scent that led to the strange ball of spines.

"Don't touch it," growled the mother. "You will get hurt if you do."

But the cub had his nose to the ground. He liked the smell of this strange little animal; surely it must be good to eat.

"Come away," growled Mother Bear again. "You can't eat such things."

But Baby Bear did not heed. Going closer to the ball, he gave a quick snap. Poor Baby Bear! His soft little nose, lips, and mouth were filled with sharp quills. With loud squeals and howls of pain he ran back and forth through the woods.

The young porcupine again drew in his spines and finished his evening

meal in peace; but it was many days before the little bear got rid of the troublesome quills.

THE TALE OF A GRAY RAT

Of all the rats for miles around Whiskers was the quickest, the strongest, the most daring. He could run faster and jump higher than any of them.

He was fond of all good things to eat, but the thing he liked best of all was cake.

His home was a small, round room with a long hall. On one side of the room was a soft nest, made of bits of hay, and lined with tiny pieces of paper. Here the five Whisker babies slept and ate; they were too little to do anything else. The hall went down into the ground for a long way, and then up, with its front door under the cellar steps. Whiskers had chosen this place for a home because there was always plenty of cake in the cellar.

The people who lived in the house wished that Whiskers would go somewhere else. They were fond of cake too, but they didn't like it nibbled or with great pieces bitten out. So they tried to get rid of him."

One night the rat found a tempting piece of meat on the shelf. He was hungry for meat, so he went to it. He stopped and sniffed at it. He could smell something else besides meat, something that he had

smelled before. At first he could not think what it was; then all at once he remembered. When he was a very young rat his mother had said to him, "Never eat anything that smells like that; if you do, it will kill you. It killed your father."

When the people in the house found that Whiskers had not touched the meat, they said, "The rat doesn't like meat; we will put the poison on some cake." They did, but Whiskers smelled the same smell and wouldn't even taste it. He began to understand that the people in the house wished to kill him, so he was careful to test everything before he ate.

One night not long after, he saw a cat on the stairway. The cat kept still when she saw him and waited for him to come out.

"Oho!" laughed Whiskers, "not yet; just wait awhile." Then he called five of his friends, and together they went to the cellar.

The cat jumped for the first rat, and the four others jumped for her. They bit her ears and face until she fled to the top of

the steps and stayed there, too frightened to move.

Then the rats had a big feast. They nibbled or carried away everything that was on the shelf.

"There is only one thing we can do," said the people of the house; "we'll get a dog."

The next day Whiskers heard a great barking in the cellar. He ran along his hall as far as he dared and looked. A dog was digging at the hole under the cellar steps and barking.

"What is it?" asked Mrs. Whiskers.

"We'll have to move," said Whiskers; "I can't fight a dog."

Mrs. Whiskers was trembling all over; the barking of the dog had so frightened her.

"Let us go tonight," she said. And they did.

THE MERRY MICE

The merry mice stay in their holes,
    And hide themselves by day;
But when the house is still at night
    They all come out to play.

They climb upon the pantry shelf,
    And taste of all they please —
They drink the milk that's set for cream.
    And nibble bread and cheese.

But if they chance to hear the cat,
    Their feast will soon be done —
They'll scamper off to hide themselves,
    As fast as they can run.

Some tiny mice live in the fields,
    And feed on flies and corn,
And in a pretty hanging nest
    The little ones are born.

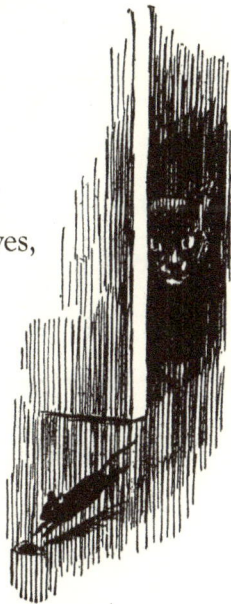

When winter comes they burrow holes,
    And line them soft with hay;
And while the snow is on the ground
    They sleep the time away.

                — SELECTED

GNAWERS

beaver	hare	squirrel
porcupine	rabbit	prairie dog

The gnawers are so called because they have four sharp, chisel-shaped teeth that are specially fitted for gnawing through hard substances. Their food consists principally of bark, the roots of trees, woody stems, and even nuts and stony seeds. The animals of this family are weak and timid. They seldom fight an enemy, but depend upon saving themselves by running away. These animals are also called rodents.

The beaver is one of the largest animals of this group. It shows a wonderful instinct in constructing a dam in the stream or river near which it makes its home. Many beavers work together in forming these dams, which are composed of logs, the branches of trees, stones, and mud.

The body of the porcupine is covered with sharp quills, which can be extended or drawn back into its soft fur. It eats fruit, bark, roots, and the leaves of many plants.

The hare does not live in a burrow as the rabbit does, but makes a nest among the dry grass and leaves. Hares frequently injure young trees and often destroy the crops of the farmer by nibbling the tender blades of wheat and other grain.

The rabbit is smaller than the hare but closely resembles it in form. It lives in burrows which it digs in the ground. The mother rabbit forms a soft nest at the end of the burrow composed of hay, dry leaves, and fur torn from her body. Here the young rabbits are kept until they are strong enough to care for themselves.

The squirrel is one of the most beautiful of our small animals. It has bright eyes, soft fur, and a bushy tail. It makes its home in the hollow trunk of a tree, where it lays away a store of food for winter.

The prairie dog is found on the western plains. A number of them live together and make their homes in burrows.

Other members of this family are the rat, mouse, muskrat, guinea pig, field mouse, chipmunk, gopher, flying squirrel, and woodchuck.

VI.
THE MONKEY FAMILY

THE SICK MONKEY

Away in the forest in Africa the mother monkey and her young one had been caught in a trap. The struggles of the mother and the cries of the little one did not save them. They were placed in a large basket and carried on the back of a man many miles to the seashore, where there was a great ship.

There the monkeys were taken from the basket and placed in a box with bars across the front. Greatly frightened, the mother held her little one in her arms and tried to hide him from the curious people who came to look at them.

On board the ship, the box was placed in a low, dark room under the deck. For weeks the ship was rocked and tossed by the waves, and down under the deck the mother monkey still held her little one.

At last the big engines stopped. People passed to and fro on the deck and into the hold, and the box was taken up into the sunshine again.

Here was a new and strange world. The little

monkey trembled, and the frightened mother hugged him closer.

A wagon came and carried them away through the crowded streets. Between the bars the mother could see great piles of stone, yet they were not like the rocks on the mountains. She drew back in the far corner of the box and turned away from the strange sights.

At last the wagon stopped inside the gates of a big park.

" Here, keeper," called the driver, "here are the new monkeys you have been so anxious about."

A man came quickly to the side of the wagon.

"The big one is fine," he said, "but the little one does not seem well. The long sea voyage has been too hard for him. We will put them into the big cage at once."

The bars were opened, and the monkeys were in their new home. Other monkeys were chasing each other, swinging from bars, and eating nuts and fruit. A few of them stopped their play to look at the newcomers. Two or three chattered to them, but the mother did not heed. Anxiously she watched her little one. He lay with his eyes closed and did not move even when the keeper came again to see them.

In the corner of the cage was soft straw, and here the mother fixed a bed. For two days the little fellow lay there or was carried in his mother's arms.

Then one morning he opened his eyes and looked about him. The sun was shining, and the world was bright and beautiful. Slowly he climbed out of his bed and crept across the floor. By the side of the cage was the keeper, who offered him a choice bit of food.

This man was a strange creature to the little monkey from Africa, but the other monkeys did not seem

to be afraid of him. Even the mother took things from his hand.

The little fellow slipped up to his mother's side, and then he too took a piece of the tempting food. It was good, so good that he took another piece, and still another.

Then he sat in the sunshine and watched the other monkeys swing and play on the highest bars. The mother ventured to leave him a few minutes while she talked with an old monkey in the next cage. Each day brought good food and bright sunshine for the young one, and each day gave him new strength.

The next week a frisky little monkey chased his mother up one side of the cage and down the other, chattered and played with the monkeys, and begged for nuts and fruit from the boys and girls who came to watch him.

"The little one is all right now," said the keeper. "He is the brightest, cutest monkey in the park."

GREEDINESS

One Saturday afternoon, Ralph's father took him to the Park to see the animals.

There were lions, tigers, bears, elephants, seals, and many other kinds of animals, but what pleased the boy most was the monkeys.

Ralph had a bag of peanuts, which the monkeys must have smelled, for they reached out their hands, expecting to be fed.

One big monkey reached out farther than the rest, and just as Ralph was about to give him a peanut, he snatched the whole bagful and ran off with it as fast as he could go.

Then the fun began. All the other monkeys began to chase him, up and down the sides of the cage, across the top, then to the top of the big bare tree that stood in the middle of the space.

All this time the big monkey held the peanuts so tight in his paw, that by and by there came a little hole in the bottom of the bag. It grew and grew until there was a large hole where the little one had been. First one peanut fell, then another, and another, until there was none left in the bag.

Down below, the monkeys were having a feast, scrambling over each other as monkeys do, pushing each other out of the way, as long as the peanuts continued to fall.

The greedy monkey had been running so fast that be knew nothing of what was going on. At last he sat down on a bar at the top of the cage to eat his peanuts. Slowly he opened the bag, grinning as he thought of the fine treat he was to have, but to his surprise there wasn't a peanut left; nothing but a paper bag with a hole in it!

— Adapted from *Primary Education*

THE MONKEY FAMILY

gorilla   orangutan

chimpanzee   baboon

These animals can
use both hind feet
and front feet as hands,
and so are known as "four-
handed animals." They are
sometimes called "man-
shaped animals," because their shape
and actions are somewhat like those of
human beings. They feed on nuts, fruits,
and other vegetable food. Some members of this family are found in nearly all
warm countries. The gorilla is the largest

and strongest animal of this group. It lives in the thick jungles of Africa and is so ferocious that it will attack a man.

The chimpanzee is also found in Africa. It lives on the ground and spends much of its time under rocks and in caves. When captured, this animal may be taught to perform many acts like those of a human being.

The orangutan is found in the warm parts of Asia. It makes its home in the tops of trees, where it forms nests or seats by weaving the branches together. Its arms are long and strong and are adapted for climbing. When angry it is exceedingly fierce, but a young orangutan is gentle, and like the chimpanzee may be easily trained.

The baboon is sometimes called "the dog-headed monkey" because its head is much like that of a dog. Baboons live in large bands and together make a fierce attack upon any enemy that comes against them.

While all the animals of this group may be spoken of as monkeys, yet this term is usually given to the smaller members. These active little creatures live in the tree tops and feed on fruit, nuts, insects, and small birds. Some of them use their tails to aid them in climbing trees and in swinging from bough to bough. The tail seems to answer the purpose of a fifth hand and is used in many ways.

VII.
THICK-SKINNED
ANIMALS

PUTTING A BABY ELEPHANT
TO BED

It was getting dark in the big circus tent, and Nellie kept close to her father as they walked across the great ring where the animals performed. In the animals' tent a gasoline light fluttered and smoked in the wind.

"You're just in time," said the circus man.

In one corner of the tent were several elephants.

One mother elephant had a baby elephant not much taller than Nellie.

"She'll put her baby to bed pretty soon," said the circus man. "She always does before it's time to go into the ring for the evening performance."

Nellie and her father sat down on a bale of straw and watched the great gray beasts as they ate their supper.

Presently the mother elephant put her trunk around the baby's neck, and seemed to whisper to him as he rubbed his head against her knee. He stood still a moment, then raised his head,

flapped his little ears, and trotted off by his mother's side to a corner of the pen.

There she left him and went to a pile of hay nearby. She took up bunch after bunch of it with her trunk and spread it round her baby. The baby did not once stir from the spot where she had left him.

When the hay was all spread, the mother began to tread it down with her feet. Then she went to the farther side of the pen and fumbled about the ground with her trunk.

This time she stood out-side the baby's bed, and blew

a cloud of fine dust into the folds of his skin, till he was thoroughly powdered for the night.

After a few soft pats and a few soft grunts from his mother, the baby lay still and was soon fast asleep.

But Mamma Elephant's work was not yet done. She took up hay in her trunk and tossed it lightly along the baby's sides and back until he was entirely covered.

"What did she do all that for?" asked Nellie.

"In the elephant's home in India and Africa," replied her father, "there are many big snakes which might harm the little one.

In the forest she makes the baby's bed of grass and leaves and treads it down to make sure there are no snakes hidden in it. When she makes the bed of hay in this country she does the same thing. She blew dust on him because in their home insects get into the tender folds of the baby's skin and bite him; the dust keeps them out. And the mother covered him up so that no hunter could find him. In their own home she would have covered him with leaves, sticks, and grass."

THE DOCTOR AND THE ELEPHANT

Jack had run a thorn into his foot and it pained him so that he could hardly step. But when Uncle Henry wanted to cut the thorn out, Jack said, "No," for he was afraid the sharp knife would hurt.

"I shall have to tell you a story about an elephant," said Uncle Henry.

Jack loved stories; so, forgetting his sore foot, he sat down to listen.

"Hebe was a fine big elephant," began Uncle Henry, "worth a great deal of money to her owner. In some way she stepped upon a nail or a sharp piece of iron, which worked into the tender part of her foot and festered. Poor Hebe was nearly wild with pain.

"A doctor was sent for, and when he came, he found Hebe swinging the hurt foot and making loud cries. He was afraid to go near her, for he knew that she could easily kill him, but the keeper told him not to fear, as the great animal would not hurt him. Very carefully the doctor took hold of the injured foot to examine it.

" 'I shall have to cut, and cut

deep,' the doctor said after he had looked at it.

"The keeper said some strange words to the elephant and then called out, 'Cut away.'"

"And did he cut?" asked Jack.

"Yes, but the first cut was not enough, and he asked the keeper, 'Shall I cut again?' "

" 'Cut again,' "was the answer.

"This time he reached the abscess. Hebe gave a long sigh of relief and stood still while the doctor sprayed and bound up her foot."

"I know what you mean," said Jack. "I suppose a boy ought to be as brave as an elephant. You may take out the thorn."

When this had been done and the sore place dressed, Uncle Henry said, "Now I will tell you the last part of the story. A year and a half later the doctor happened to be where Hebe was and asked about his patient.

" 'She is well and happy,' her keeper told him. 'Come in and see her.'

"The doctor wondered if she would know him. At first the big elephant did

not notice him, then she looked at him steadily and with interest.

Next she reached out her trunk and touched his shoulder and hair. Then she slowly lifted her great foot, now healed and sound, and showed it to him as if to say, 'You see, I remember very well what you did for me.'"

THICK-SKINNED ANIMALS

elephant   hippopotamus

rhinoceros   swine

Although the animals of this group differ greatly in size and shape, they are alike in some respects. Their bodies are heavy and are covered with a tough, thick skin. They usually live near ponds or streams and spend much of their time wallowing in the mud or standing in the water.

The elephant is the largest known land animal. It has a heavy body, stout legs, a large

head, and a long trunk. On each side of the trunk are two short horns called tusks. From these tusks fine ivory is obtained. The trunk serves the elephant in many ways. By means of it the big animal can reach into the branches of trees to pick nuts and fruit; with it the elephant breathes and smells; water is sucked through it and poured down the huge throat; it serves as a hand in picking a blade of grass, in carrying heavy loads, and in uprooting trees. Elephants can be taught to work and are often given tasks where great strength is required. They live in Southern Asia and in Africa.

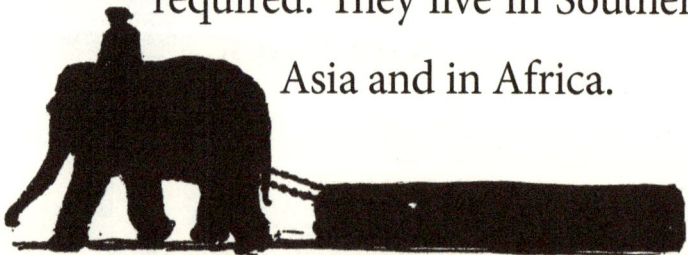

The rhinoceros has one and sometimes two horns, extending upward from the nose or upper lip. The skin of this animal is so thick that only large and heavy bullets will pierce it. Like many other animals living in hot countries, it sleeps during the greater part of the day and goes in search of food during the cool of the evening.

The hippopotamus is a huge, unwieldy creature sometimes measuring fourteen feet in length. It lives in Africa, where it is found in the river courses and along the muddy banks. Its food consists chiefly of grass and water plants, which it consumes in great quantities. The mother hippopotamus carries her little one on her neck when swimming and diving.

The swine or hog once lived in a wild state in the woods of Europe and Asia. Now it is one of our valuable domestic animals. It eats both vegetable and animal food. By means of a projection on its snout it digs roots from the ground. Its flesh is used for food; from its bristles fine brushes are made.

VIII.
CUD CHEWERS

ZARA, THE CAMEL

Zara was a young camel, very young indeed she sometimes seemed, although she was nearly as large as her mother. For four years she had played in an awkward way around the little village in Arabia where her owner lived.

Some changes had come in the last two months. She was not allowed to run around so much. Her master had begun training her, teaching her to kneel down when he said a certain word, and to remain on the ground until a load was strapped upon her back. At first Zara refused to carry the load, but after much coaxing she was made to go a little distance.

"We will take her with us on our next journey," said her master. "She is old enough now to do some work."

Zara was then put with the other camels, and for several days they were given all the food they could eat, until the humps on their backs became much larger.

Then one day the owner came to look at them. "The camels are in fine shape," he said. "I never saw them look better. See how fat they are and

how large their humps are. They can go many days without food. We will start tonight. It is too hot to travel in the daytime."

That afternoon when the loading began, all the camels knelt as Zara had been taught to do.

"We will not put a heavy load on this one," said the master as he patted Zara's head. "She is a young camel. This is her first trip."

That night as soon as the moon rose they started. Away they went in a long line across the sand. Zara, loaded with

two precious bags of water, followed close behind her mother.

Next morning a stop was made; the loads were taken from the camels and they were allowed to rest. This was not like playing around the village with the other young camels, and Zara began to wish that she were back at home. But she was a grownup camel now; at least so her master had said, and she could not always play.

Three nights they traveled and three days they rested. Then the master said: "We shall reach one of the wells tomorrow. There we can fill the bags again, and the camels can have water."

Next morning when they stopped, one of the men said: "Here is the well, but I cannot draw any water. It is dry."

"We have but a little water left in our bags," said another. "What shall we do?"

"Divide the water among the men," said the master. "The camels will have to do without. Tomorrow we shall reach a well that is never dry. Then the camels can drink all they want."

The camels were thirsty, for they had

been given no water since leaving their home in the village. That morning they wandered about, vainly trying to find a leaf or a blade of grass to eat. About noon, one of the men gave a loud cry and pointed to a yellow cloud not far away. Instantly the camels threw themselves flat on the ground, stretched their long necks as far as possible, and lay quite still. The men lay down beside them, hiding their faces in the camels' long hair; and there they stayed until the great sand storm had passed. For an hour the hot,

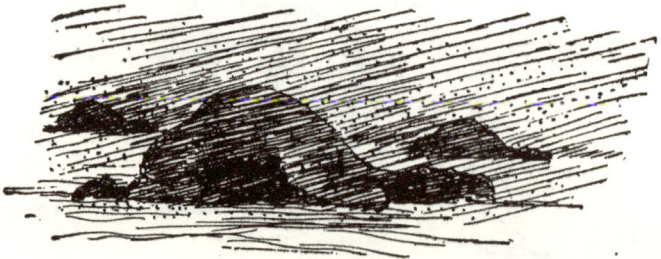

stinging sand blew all about them. With eyes, ears, and even their noses closed, the camels waited until the wind ceased. Then they rose, shook the sand from their heads and shaggy coats, and were ready for their journey.

But they were thirsty, very thirsty. The older ones sniffed the air, but found no trace of water.

Early next morning one of the men called, "This is the place of the well, for here are the trees, but where is the well?"

"It is covered with sand," said the master. "The storm of yesterday has covered it. We must dig for it."

Anxiously the men began digging with spades and shovels, but no well could be found.

"Try again," cried the master. "We must have water or we shall die."

Again the men tried, and again they found only the soft, shifting sand.

"It is of no use," said the men. "We cannot find it. We must go on. Perhaps the camels can find water for us."

Poor Zara was nearly dead, but she was obliged to go on with the rest. Slowly the line moved across the desert. The camels, with their heads hanging low, seemed almost too weak to move.

In the afternoon a change came over them. Their heads were lifted higher; some of them began to run. Joyful shouts came from the men: "We are saved! The camels will find water! "

The camels ran faster and faster. Even Zara felt new life that she could not understand.

For half an hour the race continued, and then the leaders stopped; for there before them, near a great rock, was a little stream of water!

THE MOTHER DEER
AND HER LITTLE ONE

The little deer lay in his bed of leaves under the spreading branches of the fir tree and looked out at the bright sunshine in the valley. The mother deer stood close by his side. Once in a while she stooped to lick the spotted, furry coat of the baby, then moved a few feet away as if coaxing him to come.

After several trials the little deer staggered to her, his thin legs seeming almost too weak to support his trembling body.

Slowly the mother led him down the valley, stopping every few steps while she ate the fresh grass or nibbled the leaves from the bushes and trees.

On the side of the hill other deer were feeding. Here were mother deer with young fawns, and stately father deer with great branching antlers. As the mother with the new baby joined the herd, one or two deer stopped feeding long enough to look at them, but the others seemed to take no notice.

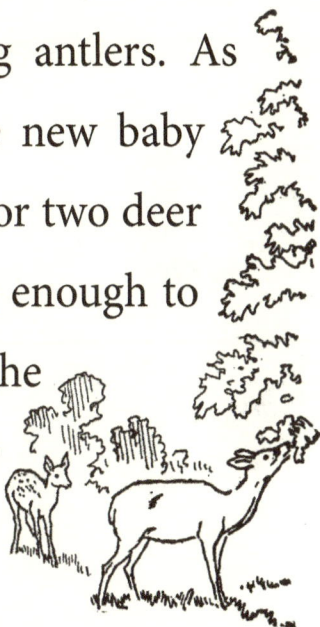

For weeks mother and fawn roamed over the green hills, drinking from the river that ran through the valley, or resting in the shade of the trees that grew along its edge. The little deer wandered by his mother's side or played with the other fawns of the herd.

The days were long and pleasant there on the shady hillside, but life in the woodland was not without its dangers. Once when the mother and fawn had wandered to the lower end of the valley, the dogs had chased them. The run was long and hard, for the mother was compelled

to slacken her pace to keep with her little one, but at last the dogs were left behind.

Another time a panther leaped from a tree and fastened its claws and teeth in the back of the mother. Rushing under the low branches of a tree, she had brushed the animal off; but it was a long time before the wounds healed.

When the fall days came the grass died, the leaves fell from the trees and bushes, and it was necessary for the herd to separate to find food. Then the mother deer showed her young one how to find the tender roots of plants under the soft earth, and

taught him to strip the bark from the trunks of young trees.

The fawn was now nearly as large as his gentle mother. The spots were beginning to disappear from his furry sides, and he looked more like the handsome father deer of the herd. During his short life he had learned much of the ways of the woods. He knew that some animals were friends of deer but that others were bitter enemies. His keen senses of smell and hearing warned him when any foe was near and his swift feet

had many times carried him far from danger.

One night, as the two deer were lying at the foot of the hill, they heard a strange noise in the valley. Both raised their heads and listened. Again the sound came, this time a long, low howl. The mother well knew what this meant; it was the cry of a pack of wolves who sometimes came there to hunt. She sprang quickly to her feet, and, closely followed by the young one, she dashed through the bushes. The howling of the wolves became

louder. The pack were on the trail, coming closer and closer!

Faster and faster the deer ran, leaping over rocks and bushes, bounding over ditches and fallen logs; but nearer and nearer came the hungry pack of wolves.

The young one began to grow tired. He had not the strength of his mother and could not endure the long run. She saw that he was going slower, and that the leader of the pack was almost up to him. Unless she could save him she knew that in a moment the cruel teeth of the leader would be fastened into his sides.

Suddenly she turned and ran straight toward the river. The young one followed, and close behind him came the greedy pack.

A few more leaps and the mother had reached the sandy shore; then she gave a great bound that took her far out into the water. A moment more, and the young one was with her, swimming toward the other side; while behind, on the river's bank, a pack of hungry wolves howled at them and snarled at each other.

CUD CHEWERS

cow	deer	bison
sheep	camel	antelope
goat	giraffe	reindeer

Cud chewers have no front teeth on the upper jaw, but their other teeth are large and strong. They have cloven hoofs; that is, their hoofs are divided into two parts. Instead of one stomach, these animals have four. The food passes into the first stomach without being chewed; after passing through the second stomach it returns to the mouth, and the animal "chews its cud." After being chewed for some time the food passes to the third and fourth stomachs.

The cow is one of the most useful animals. It gives milk from which butter and cheese are made. When it is killed, its flesh is called beef; the fat is made into candles and soap; the skin, is tanned and made into leather for boots and shoes; glue is made from the hoofs; from the horns are made buttons, combs, and the handles of knives and forks; the hair is mixed with lime to make mortar.

The sheep is about the size of a large dog. Its body is covered with a thick coat of wool, which keeps the sheep warm during the winter months. In the spring the owner cuts the wool off so that the sheep will not suffer from heat during the summer. This wool is sent to the factory, where it is woven into cloth. From the sheep's skin, soft leather is made.

The goat is much like the sheep, but instead of being covered with wool it has a thick coat of hair. Fine cloth and beautiful shawls are sometimes made from this hair. In some places the people drink the milk of the goat or make butter and cheese from it. Its skin is made into fine leather from which shoes and gloves are manufactured. Goats can climb up the rocky sides of hills and mountains where few other animals can go.

The deer is not so large as the cow. The father deer has fine horns or antlers ; these drop off every year and new ones grow. The deer is timid and is a swift runner.

The camel is called "the ship of the desert." Instead of hard, horny hoofs it has broad, flat feet that do not sink into the soft sand. It can carry a heavy load and can go long distances without food or water. Before starting on a long journey it is given a large quantity of food. This causes the hump on its back to become much larger. When it is out in the desert and no food is to be had, the fat from this hump is absorbed into the body. It lives in the deserts of Asia and Africa.

The giraffe is found in South Africa. Its long neck enables it to feed on the tender leaves of trees. It defends itself by rapid kicks with its hind legs. These kicks are so powerful that the giraffe is sometimes able to drive away even a lion.

Great herds of bison, or buffaloes, as they are called, once roamed over the western plains of America, but such large numbers of them have been killed by hunters that only a few remain. The wigwams of the Indians were often made from the hides of these animals.

The antelope of America is called the Rocky Mountain sheep or goat, in many respects it resembles the deer, but differs from it in the shape of its horns.

The reindeer is found in the cold lands of the north. It is used as a beast of burden and taught to draw a sledge with a heavy load. Its flesh is used for meat and from its skin warm clothing is made.

Other animals belonging to this group are the moose, elk, llama, chamois, and musk ox.

IX.
THE HORSE FAMILY

BUCEPHALUS

Bucephalus, the most famous horse that ever lived, belonged to Alexander the Great.

He had been raised by a man who loved beautiful horses. For a long time the man kept the horse because no one would pay the high price he asked. At last the king, Alexander's father, heard of it and asked that Bucephalus be brought to the palace. "

So one morning the owner led the horse into the palace

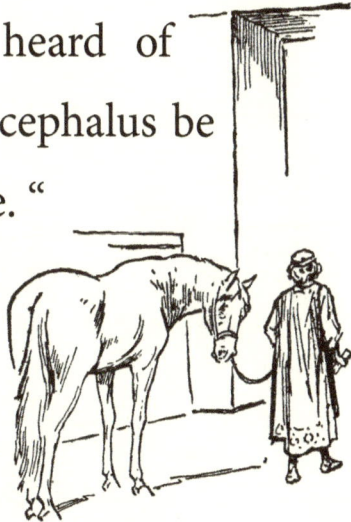

grounds. The king and all his nobles crowded round to look at it. Never before had such a beautiful animal been seen.

"Behold this wonderful horse," said the owner. "Is he not splendid? He is fit for a king."

"He is pleasing to look at," replied the king. "I should like to own him; but first I would see one of my men ride him."

A man from the stables approached the horse and attempted to mount him. Bucephalus reared upon his hind feet, and the man was thrown off. Another man tried, this time

one of the finest riders in the kingdom. Again the horse refused to carry any one on his back. Others tried with the same result.

"Take the horse away," said the king. "He is vicious. No one can ride him."

Now, the boy Alexander was standing by his father's side and had been eagerly watching all that occurred.

"Oh, Father," he cried, "don't send such a beautiful horse away. Those men do not know how to manage him."

The king was surprised at the boy. "Do you think you know more than these older and wiser men ?" he asked.

"I may not be wiser than they," replied the boy, "but I know I could ride this horse."

The king and his nobles laughed loudly at this.

"Please let me try," begged Alexander. "If I fail I will pay you the price of the horse."

Then Alexander went up to Bucephalus and taking him by the bridle turned his face toward the sun so that he could not see his own shadow. The boy had noticed that the horse seemed afraid whenever he saw his shadow on the ground. Alexander petted him and spoke gently to him. Then suddenly he leaped upon his back. Bucephalus seemed surprised; he made one effort to throw his young rider, then turning he ran swiftly down the road. When the end of the course was reached, Alexander turned the horse around and rode him back to the place where his father was anxiously waiting.

"Well done, my son!" cried the king. "The horse shall be yours, for you have conquered him. You have shown that you should have large dominions to rule. I fear my little kingdom will be too small for you."

Bucephalus served Alexander for many years. The horse

would not allow anyone but Alexander to ride him. If a groom tried to mount him, back would go his ears, and up would go his heels.

He went with his master through many wars and at last died of old age. Alexander grieved for his faithful friend. He caused a fine funeral to be made in his honor and placed over his grave a large monument bearing the one word: BUCEPHALUS

THE STORY OF A DONKEY

Some time ago, there was a poor man in Spain who made a living by selling milk. He lived in the country and sold his milk in the town. Every day he carried the milk to the houses of the people, just as the milkmen do in this country. He had a long way to go and many days he came home very tired.

One day he said to his wife, "I must have some help with my work. The load is too heavy for me to carry."

"If you only had a donkey," said his wife, "h e could carry the milk bottles for you."

"Yes," said he, "a donkey would be a great help to me; but how am I to get one? We have no money to spare."

They often talked about the donkey, and at last made up their minds to save every penny they could to buy one.

The milkman worked harder than ever. Every day he put away a little money until at last the donkey was bought.

It was a happy day for the poor man when he brought the animal home and showed him to the family. The children were delighted. They gathered around him, called him all kinds of pet names, and patted him with their hands. They thought that they had never seen so fine a donkey anywhere.

The milkman's work was now much easier, for the donkey carried the bottles of milk in two big sacks which hung across his back, while his master walked at his side. Thus they were able to take out more milk to sell, call at more houses, and so make more money.

The donkey soon became a great pet with the children; he was so gentle that the little ones played with him as if he had been a great dog.

Day after day the milkman and his donkey went their daily round, and called at the same houses to sell milk. In this way many months passed, and the donkey became as well known as his master.

One day the milkman was not well, but he went his round and got along as best he could. That night he was worse. In the morning he was so ill that he could not leave his bed.

"What was to be done? His wife could not go with the donkey. She was needed at home to nurse her sick husband. None of the children could go; they were all too young. If the milk was not sold, it would spoil and be lost. Then, the milk-man knew that the people could not do without the milk.

His wife said: "We will send the don-key to town with the milk. He is a clever fellow. The people will know him. They will help themselves to the milk."

Then she packed the bottles of milk in the large bags which hung from the donkey's back. When all was ready, she started the animal on the road he had so often taken with his master.

The donkey walked away. The milkman had never used a whip or stick to drive him along. The don-key did not know

why he was going alone. He only knew that he had been told to go by those who had always been kind to him.

The mother and children stood at the cottage door and watched the donkey out of sight. Then they went inside to care for the sick man.

The donkey marched on, going just as fast as if his master had been by his side. He seemed to know that he had the work to do alone. He never took a wrong turning. He did not stop once to eat grass by the way.

At last he reached the town. There he walked straight to the first house a which his master sold milk; the door wa shut and no one came to him. Then he seemed to remember what his master pulled the rope which hung at each door. Taking it in his mouth, the donkey gave it a pull. The door opened and someone came out to him.

To get around as quickly as possible, the milkman had often left the donkey at one door while he went on to the next. So the people were used to helping themselves.

The woman who came out took a bottle of milk and went away to empty it. The donkey waited until she brought back the empty bottle, and then he went on o the next house.

Soon the people in the street saw what he was doing. They thought that the milkman must be ill, and they were surprised and pleased to see how well the donkey could do the work alone. Some of them patted him and gave him bread and cake to eat.

All this time the milkman was thinking about the donkey. He knew that the faithful animal would do his best. He did not think that anyone would bother him, and he could trust all the people to take only their own milk. He was afraid, however, that the donkey would not remember all the houses at which he

should call. Or perhaps he would return home before he had completed his round.

But the donkey knew the last house as well as the first. As soon as he had called there, he went no farther. Without a word from any one he turned about and started for home.

The milkman felt a little better that afternoon, so he sat outside the door to watch for the donkey's return. He had not been there long, when he saw his faithful servant trotting along the road. In a few minutes the donkey had reached his master.

There in the bags were the empty bottles all safe and sound. Not one was missing or broken! The donkey had, indeed, done his work well.

THE HORSE FAMILY

horse   donkey

burro   zebra

The animals of the horse family have one hoofed toe on each foot. The hair on their bodies is short and smooth, but their manes and tails are long and bushy. They feed chiefly on grain, grass, and the leaves of plants. When wild they live in herds.

The horse is the largest domestic animal. It has a long body, an arched neck, and long, slender legs. Its ears are pointed and its eyes are large and bright. It is a faithful servant to man and worthy of his greatest care and protection.

The donkey is much like the horse in shape, but it has a longer and thicker coat of hair, and its ears are much larger.

The burro is smaller than the donkey. It can climb up the steep sides of mountains where other beasts of burden would not dare to go.

The zebra roams over the plains of southern Africa. The body of this beautiful animal is covered with brown stripes. It has long, pointed ears, small hoofs, and a long tail. It is wild and extremely difficult to capture.